THE CLASS STORE

Written By

Felecia George Prince

Copyright @ 2019 by
Felecia George Prince

All rights reserved. No part of this book may be reproduced, scanned, or distributed in any printed or electronic form or by any means without prior written consent of the publisher, except for brief quotes used in reviews.

Please do not participate in or encourage piracy of copyrighted materials in violation of the author's rights. Purchase only authorized editions.

Library of Congress Control Number
2019908679
ISBN 978-1-950894-03-1

Printed in the United States of America

This book is dedicated to all of those who taught me that it's better to give than to receive.

Thank you, God!

Thank you, Momma and Daddy!

Dear Readers,

Thank you for buying and reading my first book. I hope you will find it motivating and useful. I truly thank God for speaking to my heart. Feel free to use any of the ideas shared in this book. I do hope and trust before you choose to reprint in efforts of making a profit, you would, in respect, contact me for that permission. Again, thank you so much and Happy Reading!

Contents

INTRODUCTION 7

HISTORY 11

THE REAL GAME OF SHOW, THEN TELL 13

THE QUESTIONS KIDS ASK 21

CHAPTER 1 24
WHAT CAN I BUY IN THE STORE?

CHAPTER 2 34
WHEN WILL THE STORE OPEN?

CHAPTER 3 49
DO I NEED MONEY? TICKETS? WHAT TICKETS?

CHAPTER 4 56
HOW DO I GET TICKETS OR BUCKS TO BUY THINGS?

CHAPTER 5 61
HOW MANY TICKETS AND BUCKS WILL I NEED TO BUY THINGS?

CHAPTER 6 66
FINES? WHAT ARE FINES? WHEN DO I
PAY THE FINE?

CHAPTER 7 82
THE STORE IS OPENED? CAN I SHOP?
IT'S SHOPPING DAY?

CHAPTER 8 92
THE STORE IS CLOSED? WHEN WILL IT
OPEN AGAIN?

"THE CLASS STORE RAP" 97

SUMMARY 100

ABOUT THE AUTHOR 101

Introduction

I just love giving to others. In Acts 20:35, the words are found, "It is more blessed to give than to receive." I have always tried to live and teach by these words. **"THE CLASS STORE"** is a symbol of my belief. It captivated the soul of my discipline plan as a teacher.

Many students in our classes do the right things daily. They are listening, staying on task, being respectful, and following rules. But unfortunately, these students are frequently overlooked as a teachers' attention is so consumed with numerous discipline issues from other students that are off task, disrupting class, distracting others, disrespectful, and displaying negative acts. Interestingly enough, many students with inappropriate behaviors may end up with more incentives. You may be asking, "How can this be?" Simple, teachers may give some students with chronic behavior an abundance of incentives in order to stimulate improved behavior from those students.

Incentivizing in the classroom isn't a bad thing. I love it! I believe it can motivate some of those "Intensive Care Students" (ICS). I define ICS as a simulation, comparable to ICU, the Intensive Care Unit of a hospital. These students' behaviors seem to be frequently out of control. Yes, they need our immediate attention; but, as teachers, we must remember, other students also need our attention.

We must find ways not to allow those disruptive behaviors to "suck the wind out of our teaching sails" until we get so frustrated that other students are hindered. The differentiated approaches, such as implementing wonderful enrichment activities, accelerated activities, great project-based learning activities, musical activities, interactive discussions, cooperative group activities, presenting dynamic lectures, incorporating performance arts, just good teaching and storytelling and distributing wonderful treats, can be used to keep our students motivated!

We just can't allow those disruptive behaviors to control our classrooms. Notice, I said, "Disruptive behaviors" because we must be careful not to "throw the baby out with the bathwater." It's okay to throw out the dirty bath water (disruptive behavior), but we need to find ways to save the baby (the student).

I've always held to the belief and I still do, that ALL students can learn and deserve recognition some of the time. This is what I had in mind when I designed "**THE CLASS STORE**." I am so grateful to share **"THE CLASS STORE"** with you. The key to success will be staying positive, teaching how it works, giving frequent reminders, reviewing daily, and being consistent. For this unique approach to work, it must be taught. Don't assume anything!

At the end of some of the chapters, look for **Concepts in Action (CIA).** This is where I share a few suggestions on what you may use in creating your class store.

HISTORY

"**THE CLASS STORE**" idea was birthed years ago after visiting fun places with my son Jalen and nephew-son Caleb on vacation. We enjoyed hanging out at "Dave and Busters," "The Clubhouse," and "Chucky Cheeses." I especially liked the concept of receiving tickets for playing games and redeeming the tickets for prizes.

I enjoyed seeing the long stream of tickets come out of the arcade machines by professional gamers. So, I gave it a shot with my favorite arcade games, "Pac Man and Skee Ball." My stream of tickets may not have been as long, but I was happy with the "little stream of tickets" I did win. Without hesitation, I now had tickets to redeem for a PRIZE!!

My excitement didn't end after I received my prize; the real prize came in the form of a "great idea" that suddenly triggered my mind after the vacation ended. The seed was planted, and a plan grew to create "**THE CLASS STORE!**"

THE REAL GAME OF "SHOW, THEN TELL"

After spending the summer planning for the new school year, I was ready to tell my students all about **"THE CLASS STORE."** I chose not to introduce my new idea in the traditional format by lecturing, showing a PowerPoint or passing out worksheets, which are usually left on the floor for me to clean up afterwards. Instead I had another plan, one I knew would be eye-catching, mouthwatering, and attention-keeping for years to come. I was excited! I could hardly wait for that school day!! I knew it was going to be AWESOME!!

The day came, and I did my usual routine of meeting and greeting students at the door. As students entered my classroom, I knew it was only a matter of time before I received questions. I portrayed a sense of normalcy as students arrived. "Good morning!" "HELLO!" "So nice to see you today!" "So glad you chose to come to class!" "Welcome to my class!" "Students, you will find items on your desk and a message with instructions on the board. You may choose a seat. Again, I am so glad you are in my class this year."

Purposely, I did not mention the store when they arrived because I wanted to allow them to take the "wheel and control the conversation." I just kept a normal face and stance until the students were ready to generate the discussion.

"THE CLASS STORE" was hard to miss. I designed the store area to catch their attention. It was colorful, festive, and inviting to the eye. There was music playing in the background that added to the atmosphere. Yes, I did all of this for many years just to motivate my students to learn and to let them know I truly cared about them.

The classroom setting was designed to captivate their attention on the first day! I was preparing my students to learn, and each year they learned more than just social studies. They learned "real life" lessons.

"Welcome to PRINCEMART!!" These words extended high above the store area written on a poster board. "We count tickets, NOT cash!"

The area was stocked with long tables of treats, such as cookies, candies, chips, drinks, school supplies, toys, book bags, cell phone holders, games, clothing items, gift cards, home supplies, shoes, and so much more I thought students would enjoy and be motivated to buy.

Well, the wait was over. It didn't take long for me to hear chatter coming from within. As I continued greeting students on the outside and monitoring the hall area, I couldn't help but hear students in curious discussions about the things in the store. Also, it was hard just to focus on the hall without looking inside. So, as I looked back and forth, I saw many students with eyes stretched wide looking at all the stuff in **"THE CLASS STORE."**

Even though most of the students just looked and talked among themselves, there was always the brave and bold one to ask the first question. "Ms. Prince, what's that for?"

Like a popcorn machine, the questions started to pop more. "Who is that stuff for?" "Are we going to eat? "Are we having a party?" Students told other students who may not have been as focused in that direction, "Look." "Look at all that stuff!" It was a LOT! The store was a BIG DEAL to me, and I wanted it to be a BIG DEAL to all of my students.

It only took one of my four classes to hear about the store before the word spread like wildfire. Those students in the first block became "little missionaries" or "little ambassadors" for **"THE CLASS STORE."**

When my other classes arrived, they had already heard the news. As the students entered, I saw their anticipation and expectation at the highest level. I heard them whispering and chatting among themselves with words such as, "That's the store.

There's a LOT of stuff. I see chips." Over the years, some students specifically looked for certain things. "I wonder if she has the "blue bag of Doritos and Takis?" "I see some Takis!" "She even has lotion. I am going to buy that!" "We are going shopping, and I am going to buy some chips." "We got to have tickets." These were some of the words and statements I heard students say.

It was always flattering to me to hear a student on the first days of school say, "Ms. Prince, you are my favorite teacher!" I responded by saying, "This is just the first day of school. I haven't taught you social studies yet." Students continued by saying, "We know, but we had already heard about you. We were hoping to be in your class." I am sure the student had also heard about **"THE CLASS STORE"** or how I gave lots of treats. It probably helped me receive some of those accolades. I was grateful to have been recognized in such a thoughtful way; however, **"THE CLASS STORE"** wasn't designed for me to "get the glory." God receives that, but it was designed because I LOVED ALL my students and I wanted to see them achieve. I didn't want to write up anyone.

I realized I taught middle school and they were going to be talkative and busy. I needed to teach and I needed them to learn. So, I worked hard on a system that helped me be successful in helping them be successful. That's what I loved about **"THE CLASS STORE."**

Designing the store to be a proactive part of my classroom management and discipline plan was a wonderful way of utilizing my focus on "Positive Discipline." I believe positive discipline works! It's like the saying,

"You can catch more flies with honey than with vinegar."

Writing up students was NOT my thing. I really hated to do write-ups, even though I knew some behaviors required one and forced me to do it. **"THE CLASS STORE"** and those tickets helped me to write up a very minimal number, and most years, I counted the number of write-ups on one hand, only needing three fingers at the most.

I knew there would be a lot of questions and I was ready! I used a "Backwards' Approach" to answer what probably would have been their very first question, "What can we buy?" Instead of trying to lay out a convincing picture through talking or showing them pictures, I did what I felt "captured their attention." I started with a strong message of **"SHOW, then TELL."**

THE QUESTIONS KIDS ASK

? ? ? ? ? ?

From a young age, I loved to ask questions. I thought of myself as being "quite inquisitive!" Now, if you had a conversation with my mother and grandmother back then, they would have a different way of putting it. "NO, she was just nosey," they would say.

Nosey? How could that be? Back in my much younger days trying to be nosey was somewhat a difficult task. First, as a child, you had to dismiss yourself when "grown folks" were talking. Some of you reading this book know I am right.

As a child, you just didn't join in "grown folks" conversations. Nevertheless, my "inquiring mind" still wanted to know things, so I asked a lot of questions to get a clear understanding.

The Bible says in the book of Hosea 4:6, **"My people are destroyed for lack of knowledge."** You can say, I didn't want to be **destroyed** or **perish** for a lack of knowledge, so I asked lots of thoughtful questions.

As teachers and parents, we encourage or should encourage our kids to ask questions, especially when they don't know or are unsure of answers. **"Ask before acting; think before speaking."** These are safe commands to live by.

My students held fast to this belief when they saw the store. Like a gigantic waterfall, the questions didn't stop coming and coming. **"THE CLASS STORE"** generated a lot of questions from many "inquiring minds." My students wanted to learn about the store and how to get those "tasty treats" in the store. The questions came and I was ready to answer them. I was excited! It really made teaching so much fun for me!!!

As you read, each chapter of the book uniquely starts with a question or questions students asked. These questions are the topics for each chapter in the book. Following the question is the answer they received.

Chapter 1

What Can I Buy in the Store?

Answer: "All the items you see and more."

Many of our students are visual learners! There is a saying, "If you tell me, I'll forget; but, if you show me, I will remember." I designed the presentation of the store in efforts to capture the students' attention from the start!

Visualization is a powerful tool! I wanted to introduce a powerful system that lasted long after the students moved on and I retired.

Truly, I believe those students who experienced the store received that powerful lesson. If teachers want to teach a great lesson for students to remember, they should add some visualization. "It's good to hear a lesson; but, it's even better to see a lesson."

You may choose not to create a major store as I did. It does take some work and different energy to produce. Using differentiated methods can be time-consuming and they can require a certain creativity that involves thinking out of the box. They require some energy, but for your children, your students, it's worth it. They will be able to see the authenticity in your desire to make their learning process rewarding.

So, if you choose not to build a large store, just display items on a table or shelf. It's your choice on the methods you use, but the message will still be loud and clear that you care enough to give your very best in helping them be their best. Your creative choice will still add interest and excitement to a traditional classroom setting or any setting in general. It's what I like to call, "Reach'em Before You Teach'em."

CIA
1. Begin with "Show, then Tell." Create the store and display items that can be purchased. This is so important that "your shoppers" know what they will be working hard to buy. Food is always the number one hit. The store can include the following:

- Food treats: candy, chips, cookies, drinks, juices, Kool-Aid packs, etc.

- Beauty supplies: nice lotions (Bath and Body), hand sanitizer, nail kits and more
- Games: bingo, checkers, puzzles, baseball cards and more
- Home goods: towels, candle holders, picture frames and posters
- Clothing items: socks, flip flops, t-shirts, hats, gloves
- School supplies: pencils, pens, paper, tablets, bookbags, notebooks, gym bags.

2. Generate participation among students. Ask them to write things they would love to buy in the store. This gives students a sense of ownership or buy-in, which may encourage them to work harder to earn bucks and not create fines to lose their bucks. The store can be a great way to begin your school year during your class orientation and relationship-building techniques. Many students have great ideas if they are allowed to "share." For the Bible scholars, remember, "Jesus was only 12-years-old."

3. Everything doesn't have to cost. That's right! Yes, I spent a lot of money on items for the store. I wanted my students to have great things to buy. However, there were items that students could buy that cost nothing or very little for me to produce. Don't let money stand between your giving. Create items that students will work hard to buy, and they will cost you nothing to produce. I created a few and shared them for your use. The key is to sell the idea to them. Make the item VALUABLE! Give it worth! Use your best sales voice. Make the free pass attractive to the eye and sound like it is the BEST item since the invention of their cell phone. As teachers, or youth leaders, your attitude, enthusiasm, and motivation will EXCITE and MOTIVATE your students. I saw that in my "BBABGP."

The "BBABGP" was a "HOT ITEM" on the list back in the day. The "BBABGP" stands for *Buy Back A Bad Grade Pass*. The students knew what grades they could use it for at the beginning; however, I made it VALUABLE!! I gave it WORTH and kids bought it!! It costed me nothing except a little time to create. To add interest to the purchase, drop in a few "No cost passes," and a food item in a zip lock bag, then, add a ticket price. The kids will buy it!!" Adding food works every time!!

Below, you will find a list of passes that students will be motivated to buy that only require pen and paper. You may use these passes or create some for your class. A few of the passes are listed below:

- Free computer
- Choose your seat for the day
- Teacher assistant
- Free library
- Game
- Homework
- Beginning assignment
- Add 2 points to a daily grade
- Board writer for the day
- Free-time
- Buy back a bad grade (BBABG)
- Music listening chair
- Erase a daily grade
- Office assistant

- 5 points added to daily grade
- Skip an assignment
- Bathroom
- Water
- Locker
- Write on the board
- Artist
- Highchair
- Reading
- Bulletin board designer
- Plant care specialist
- Attendance manager
- Time-keeper manager
- Room cleaner
- Free shopping
- 5 extra tickets
- Door monitor
- Paper passer
- Pre-shopper
- 5 item buyer

- **SUPER SHOPPER**
  3 days with extra 10 tickets (for each day)
- Discount pass (1/2 off)
- Paper and pencil
- Borrow an item

4. Suggestions to furnish the items for the store. There are many other ways to possibly supply items for the store. Don't be afraid to ask and seek everywhere for wonderful items. Always add products that are necessities, such as toiletries, like toothbrushes, toothpaste, soap, lotions, combs, and brushes. Make sure all items are clean. Many of these items are located at companies and given away as freebies for souvenir bags. You may also consider the following:

- Write a grant

- Start a Go Fund Me page
- Ask large companies for freebees, like pens or pencils
- Ask local businesses
- Shop after-holiday sales
- Ask your principal
- Ask a celebrity
- Visit and shop yard sales
- Shop discount stores or markets
- Shop grocery stores
- Spend out-of-pocket
- Ask parent organizations
- Ask churches
- Host fundraisers.

CHAPTER 2

When will the store open?

Answer: "Look on the board, for signs, agenda and your calendar."

Immediately after the students saw all the things they could buy in the store, the next question was, "Ms. Prince, when does the store open?" I was bombarded with this same question almost daily. It demonstrated the motivation students had about shopping at **"THE CLASS STORE."**

I announced the dates. I put the store dates on the board, calendar and student agendas, and created signs to remind them of the store openings days. I tried to plan the openings for the store around holidays because I wanted students to learn the importance of giving to others during these times.

If Christmas was approaching, I had lots of items that reflected the season, like ornaments, mugs with candies, scarves and socks. Christmas socks were popular for the boys and girls. They loved the little trees or wreaths on the socks. Maybe I could find socks with bells, or stars; they would buy them.

During Christmas, I also had LOTS of CANDY CANES. The kids LOVED to buy boxes of candy canes. If my "money was funny," I sold the candy canes individually. They still loved them. To them, it was

"REAL" because it was "REAL" and I made it a serious matter of business. Students even had the "REAL" plastic shopping bags to put their items inside when they bought many items. This bag came in handy because I remember during one store opening, a student didn't have the mug he bought for his mother protected and it broke. He was very sad about that because I basically bought "one of a kind" items.

There were times when students asked me to gift wrap their item, or I just volunteered and placed their gifts in nice gift bags. I made their experiences real. The bags had the BIG SMILING FACE, which represented the positive discipline I implemented.

STEALING

I gave students time to place their products in their lockers, because unfortunately, there were "sticky fingers" within each classroom. Now, that was just another life lesson to learn in protecting your supplies and teaching others the consequences of stealing.

Students asked, "Ms. Prince, you aren't afraid that some students will be stealing from your store?" "Ms. Prince, someone was stealing." "Ms. Prince, you need to watch your store closely because I know someone that got some candy and some chips." Even, "Ms. Prince, you just too nice."

These were statements I heard from students time in and out; but I did NOT allow those statements to trouble me or make me stop. Actually, these statements made dynamic lecture starters, nice writing assignments, or good economic lessons.

I shared my views and take on topics they raised concerning stealing like this, "Yes, I am sure some of you know who you saw stealing. You may have been the one, but I don't have time to worry about that. You know if you are doing something wrong, you will 'reap what you sow.'" Saying this would truly churn up interests. Students would ask, "What does she mean by that?" But I always had some students come to my rescue and fight the battle. They quickly said, "Karma will get you!"

I did NOT allow the negative acts of stealing or accusations of stealing stop "**THE CLASS STORE**." In other words, I knew it was a good system and I wasn't going to let the negative side take control. I carried on and I must say, I really didn't have a lot of trouble because most of the students knew others would tell. I was respectful to NEVER charge anyone in an open forum. That would have been BAD BUSINESS. More importantly, I really believed the students valued **"THE CLASS STORE."**

I added teacher gifts in the store. I shared with the students, "Your teachers work hard. Thank them with a nice gift. Who knows, it may help you with your grades." I always had to remind them not to buy a gift for me. That wasn't always followed.

During one store opening, a student in my class bought me something. I had already reminded the students to buy for others, but he insisted. He came to me and said, "Ms. Prince, you want this?" When students tried to give me things, I ALWAYS made it A BIG, BIG DEAL!!

"For me?" I asked. "Oh wow, THANK YOU!" I always demonstrated that GREAT excitement! I was NOT faking; It was special to me. No one has to do anything nice for you.

He wanted to use his tickets to buy for me. I let him know I appreciated it!!

I said to him, "Don't you want to give it to your mother?" Well, he walked away for a very short period of time, continually circling my desk area, then he came back and said, "That's okay. You can have it." I guess that was another great reason to buy items for the store you may like. You just might get them back in the form of a gift.

School is out for Father's Day, but I still stocked the store with items for fathers, like mugs, coffee cups or signs with the words "DAD" or "Granddaddy." Valentine's Day store openings consisted of candies, chips, sweetheart chains, little trinkets with hearts, and so much more. Easter and springtime brought out great items such as the plastic eggs that I had a LOT of in my class. These plastic eggs were good for holding the

"FREE PASSES" or the "GOLDEN EGG" with a big treat! There were beautiful, bright colored items such as tissues, pencils and memo pads. Easter candy was always popular.

Back-to-school time always had a big store. It was filled with sport's items, gym bags, locker organizers, games, food and school supplies. It was so thrilling to see students using the items bought from the store. I loved it. Sometimes I acted as if I didn't know where they purchased the items. I may ask, "I like your notebook. Where did you get it?"

A few years ago, I saw one of my former students. After catching up about old times, he said to me, "Ms. Prince, do you still do the store?" This student had to be in his late 20's. I said, "YES." It was AWESOME he remembered the store! My former student went on to say, "My grandmother still has the gift I bought her on the shelf. I remember buying it from your store." As you all probably know, I was just EXCITED to hear this. I could also tell he was glad about the purchase and he could see how appreciative his grandmother was in receiving the gift. All these years, she still cherished it.

The store during Mother's Day was always large. One reason was it came during the end of the school year. I had been able to stock up on more items. Sometimes it was the last store opening and Mother's Day is just special anyway. The store was stocked with jewelry, picture frames, lotions from Bath and Body Works, what nots, items that lasted from the other stores, make-up sets, purses and so much more that moms and grandmothers would like. One of my former students shared, "I still have those red, heart-shaped baskets." She is in college now.

Over the years, parents have personally thanked me for the flowers and gifts their kids bought and gave to them from the store. I have heard and enjoyed so many stories over the years about items from the store. I wish I could remember all the stories; but, one of those stories that really touched my heart happened during my last months of my middle school teaching career. That story truly capitalized on what the store meant to me and hopefully to many of my students.

It was one of the last store openings of the school year. One of my students said, "I bought some cookies from the store and I gave the cookies to my mother for Mother's Day." My thoughts were "that was so sweet." Then, as I began to let that sweet statement settle in my mind, my vivid imagination went wild. I could not help but think about the journey of those cookies and how they became the ultimate gift for his mother.

First, this boy bought cookies that he could have eaten. Now, that really left me in AWE. He took control of his hunger pains. Did he remind himself over and over he was saving the cookies for his Mother's Day gift? Did he refuse to take a bite because he knew he had made a promise to himself? Did he curve his appetite with an extra piece of gum or sipping water during the day? Whatever method he chose to use, he had the determination to protect himself from eating those cookies.

Next, he bought the cookies with his hard-earned tickets. Like most middle school students, he loved to talk a lot in class. "Excessive Talking" racked up a LARGE fine and the bill had to be paid before shopping in **"THE CLASS STORE."** Still the student used whatever tickets he had left to buy a pack of cookies for his mother. Not just cookies, but a pack of "Grandma's Peanut Butter Cookies."

I couldn't help but imagine the journey those cookies took before they reached his mother on that early Sunday morning. First, that little pack of cookies possibly had to travel up and down the hallway, from class to class, and in and out of lockers. In those lockers, the cookies had to share whatever middle schoolers choose to put in lockers, an extra pair of tennis shoes, deodorant, a lunch box with a week old sandwich, worksheets, papers that hadn't made it home yet, homework that wasn't ever turned in, and an oversized bookbag (that had to be kept in the locker all day because it wasn't allowed in most classrooms), gym bags, and lots of clothes. I mean a LOT.

One year, I remember witnessing a student pulling out what looked like his "whole winter wardrobe" from his locker, consisting of four or five coats, shoes, hats, gloves, and pants. Now how he stuffed all that in one locker, I don't know to this day! Middle school lockers are narrow and short. There are three locker compartments stacked on top of each other. It must have been magic. I always said if those lockers could speak, they would say, "STOP PUSHING ME!" "STOP PUSHING ME!" That's how students closed "STUFFED LOCKERS," pushing with all their might.

Next, the cookies could have been attacked and eaten by hungry people throughout the day or lost on the journey. Middle schoolers love snacks. He knew in his mind, "If I leave them sitting on my desk, they will be gone. If my other teachers see me with them, they may take them from me. I got to be careful where I take them because I may lose them." This boy had to make a strategic decision on how to keep his little pack of "Grandma's Cookies" safe from all the hungry crew.

Finally, he could breathe. The school day ended and his cookies had survived! But, wait, his thoughts probably rattled throughout his mind, "You got to get them home." So, for the journey home, he possibly stashed that little pack of cookies somewhere in a side pocket or maybe the bottom of his bookbag surrounded by large books, papers, pencils, pens, and other interesting items that students carry in their bookbags. The cookies could have been smashed or punctured by a pen or pencil, but he had to keep them safe for the journey home.

Danger wasn't over for the cookies even when they arrived home. He had another big decision to make, and that was finding a place to store the cookies until that great day. He probably knew the cookies had to stay safe from harm or danger of one of his siblings finding them and eating them.

Sunday Morning arrived. It was Mother's Day and that little pack of "Grandma's Cookies" from **"THE CLASS STORE"** survived the tedious journey and now, they made an AMAZING Mother's Day gift for his mother. The mission was accomplished successfully. I can tell he was proud of this gift he gave to his mother because he took time to share. This was just one of the many beloved stories I experienced over the years from students who shopped in **"THE CLASS STORE."**

Chapter 3

Do I Need Money? Tickets?
What tickets?
"We count tickets, not cash."

$PRINCE BUCK$$$

Answer: "You will use tickets. We count tickets, not cash."

After answering the questions about the opening of the store, this only generated more questions and conversation, "Do I need money?" "No money, just tickets," I said. "What tickets? How do I get tickets?" The questions continued to flow as students anxiously searched for answers about this new phenom. I tried to lay out the facts and present the case in the most motivating way that I could.

I started out using a basic red ticket. Just in case you may be wondering why I chose red, I love using themes and symbols. To me, this set a pattern and created the path that I wanted to follow.

I had a lot going on in my classroom and those that may be reading this book and have visited my class can say, "Amen" to that. Now that's for another book.

Everything I did within my classroom had a significant meaning, even down to the zebra print I used throughout the room, on my desk, shelves, my scissors, containers, and favor candy bags. I loved the zebra print! This print reminded me to embrace the diversity within my classroom and the importance of having a differentiated mindset that ALL STUDENTS can learn. They may NOT learn in the same way. So, if I wanted to be an effective teacher, I had to recognize these differences. All my students were so important to me, regardless of race, creed, or color. I loved them and I was so glad they were in my class.

I didn't believe in just telling the students the answer. I wanted them to learn how to be critical thinkers for themselves. I took them on journeys "out and about" for a little while in hopes their "light bulbs" would come on.

Many of my students questioned my motive. "Ms. Prince, just give us the answer." I would strongly respond, "I am a teacher. I teach."

It was always easy for me to make experiences "teachable moments." I found them all around me. Mostly everything I used in my classroom had a teachable moment, including the red colored tickets.

The color red made me think of Jesus and the blood He shed on the cross. He did it because of love and salvation. I wanted my students to know that I loved them, and I wanted them to experience salvation from discipline issues and negative consequences they could receive because of the issues that may wreak havoc on their learning process.

One more love for red, it's the color of the roses we receive during special occasions like Valentines. It, too, signifies LOVE.

I also wanted to have a system of love and respect for all of my students, especially those who were seldom recognized because they always fell somewhere in the middle. They didn't get the top honors and they were not at the lowest percentile levels. They didn't exhibit disruptive and rude behavior.

They weren't even the talkative ones. They were students who made good decisions daily.

Many of these students just brought great attitudes and good work ethics daily with few recognitions. **"THE CLASS STORE"** would change that. Now, all my students had an opportunity to receive positive recognition.

I found tickets to be economical for me. I bought them by the rolls because I knew I would pass out a lot during the days, weeks, months, and year. Oh, the many stories I've heard over the years about those tickets. I even had a student share about a student that tried to use the ticket for the fair one year. I reminded them that the tickets wouldn't work for that. I heard stories like, "Momma washed my tickets in my pants. Can I still use them to shop?" My answer was always,

"Yes." Then I asked them, "Have you ever found money in your pants pocket or shirt pocket once it was washed? Could you still use it?" Again, it was making the **"THE CLASS STORE"** a real-life experience.

Even though the students pressed them out and some brought them wet, I still accepted the tickets. They had earned them, and they still served their purpose.

Even to this day, I meet former students who say, "Ms. Prince, I still got my tickets." I have suggested that they frame them after all these years. A few other teachers liked the idea of tickets and decided to use them, but they used different colors to separate our tickets.

In my later years of teaching, I used "Prince Bucks" named after, guess who? Me! I printed them in green because many students associated that color with money.

Also, I used the bucks to teach words like "currency," an economic term social studies students had to know and learn.

Chapter 4

How do I get the tickets or bucks to make purchases?

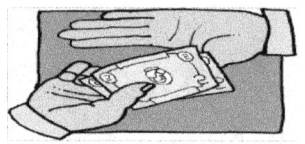

Answer: "There are multiple ways, such as coming to school, participating in class, completing assignments and being kind as well as respectful to others.

I reminded students that I could not accept cash from them, only tickets or Prince Bucks. I used an analogy of a parent's paycheck.

Students, "It is like when your parents work, they receive a paycheck for their work. Your tickets or bucks are your earnings for doing appropriate things."

Unlike their parents, students received their earnings anytime during the day. Actually, I carried rolls of tickets to lunch, in the hallways and even outdoors because I trained my eye to look for something good each student did daily.

Yes, some students ended up with hundreds of tickets and some may have ended up with a whole lot less. Treating kids equal or just alike was NOT my goal; but I made sure I treated each one fairly. I knew all my kids had differences. Some just had better work ethics than others. Some were more helpful and nicer than others. Some kids worked harder than others to earn. Some kids tried, but they lost a lot of tickets from paying too many fines. I looked for ways that every child could earn tickets.

When students received their tickets, I reminded them to place their tickets or bucks in a safe place to prevent theft. Also, I suggested they write their names on their tickets.

It was always interesting to hear, especially in team meetings, about a student having problems keeping up with class work or homework. But, he or she would have those tickets! Their tickets were not lost.

I have witnessed students using zipped pencil pouches, small containers, pocketbooks, pants pockets, wallets, student-made envelopes or little taped pockets, and more being the home for tickets. Some of my special needs students had special places in the classroom, such as a personal folder, where they kept their tickets so they would not lose them. These tickets were valuable to them. They were NOT going to lose them because they knew a shopping day was coming soon.

Some of my students asked for tickets directly, but I informed them they would have to earn bucks or tickets. Of course, some students may not earn as many as others, but I worked hard to make sure NO CHILD GOT LEFT OUT. Again, I found something good every child did so they could earn tickets or bucks if it was no more than just sitting quietly in their desks.

CIA

Here are some additional ways students can earn bucks or tickets. You may want to use these or allow these to help you generate your own ways.

    1.   Arriving on time

2. Being present
3. Saying "Thank You"
4. Helping someone
5. Working cooperatively
6. Birthday
7. Holiday gift
8. All sitting down
9. Having a pencil
10. Having paper
11. Cleaning up
12. Having the assignment
13. Smiling

CHAPTER 5

How many tickets or bucks will I need to shop?

Answer: "It depends on things you will want to buy, but things will probably not be less than 10 bucks or tickets.

I always tried to steer students away from this question and challenged them to earn all the tickets they can by doing right and making good choices. I warned them by showing them a big-ticket item, like an Under-Armor

Bag, and saying, "You need 100 bucks to buy this item."

As students gained bucks and tickets, it wasn't unusual to witness them during the day counting their stash. It seems that some just got pleasure from counting their tickets and sharing the number they had with a peer. "How many tickets do you have?" "I have 75 tickets." This seemed to be an interesting conversation for some of the students.

There were times when they had to be reminded to put their bucks or tickets away. Also, they had to be careful about having their tickets out in another class because the teacher may remove them. There were times when teachers collected students' tickets because they were out during class. Of course, the students were extremely unhappy. I did not come to their rescue. I quickly reminded them what I had warned, not to have their tickets out in other classrooms.

In the **"THE CLASS STORE,"** prices ranged from 10 to 100 bucks or tickets. It depended on the item. Because I wanted the students to learn a lesson about value and worth, I challenged them to work hard to earn bucks and tickets. I didn't actually reveal price lists until the day of the store. I asked students days before to count their tickets. Then, I generated an average cost based on tickets or bucks earned as a whole.

As in the real world, students might complain about the price being too high; but, I just informed them they must work harder to earn and not lose their tickets. Again, it was important that all students had an opportunity to earn tickets or bucks. Below are suggested ideas for setting up the cost. You can always create a system that works for your setting. Believe it or not, my students paid 20 or 40 bucks for chips. As one student said, "I got a lot of bucks!" In other words, that student had worked hard and earned bucks. I didn't ease the price.

CIA
- Consider labeling sections in the store as you see on the cover of this book: 10, 20, 40, 60, 80.
- Consider using sharpies and sticky notes to label and price items or label the various sections.

Sample Exchanges

Item	Tickets/bucks
Food (like chips)	20-40
Drinks	20-40
Small candy	10
Book bag	50

Chapter 6

FINE? What is a fine?

Answer: "A fine is the bill you pay for any marks you receive for inappropriateness."

I tried to present "fines" as a real-life lesson. "You don't need to rack up on fines. Fines will cost you and take all your hard-earned tickets or bucks." Throughout the book, you have read about students getting a fine and losing their tickets. I used a fine system for the store.

Students had to be warned that they could not shop until their fine was paid in full. **A fine is a bill created from making an inappropriate choice.** I would possibly share with them the words below:

"When your parents earn their paycheck, they may want to keep it. But they have to use it to pay bills. You will use your bucks or tickets to pay your bills. There are some bills that are required, but some are just the choices you make. For example, let's say your parent parked in a handicap parking space and didn't have a sticker on the car. If caught, they will be fined and have to pay this fine or suffer a consequence."

With daily reminders of their behavior and actions, my hope was that the students truly thought about the choices they made. I didn't have a problem working hard to remind them daily of earning tickets. I preferred to work hard at that, rather than spending my days writing up students. I used a positive discipline system instead of a negative one.

Most of the time, I did not require students to pay a bill, such as desk rent, pencil rent, or rent for the room (including lights and shelter) or creating a savings account, paying themselves. Adding these expenses possibly could have made this system even more interesting, but it would have added more responsibilities for me. Also, I believe, that even with a great system, you can overdo or overextend. As I think back now, pencil or pen rental fees would have been a great idea because students frequently needed to borrow one or the other.

Overall, more students had the opportunity to shop than not. Sadly, I saw students with too many fines and having fewer opportunities to shop; but, these same students received less write ups because there were preventions in place before sending them straight to the office. To me, it was important to save the office for students with truly severe or serious violations, such as fighting, destroying property, etc. Fortunately, I didn't have to referee many of these at all. The positive discipline system worked!

There were times when I watched some students beg others for tickets; but, immediately, I saw those students begging for tickets being rejected with words like, "You could have saved your tickets. You got all those fines. It was your fault." Now, I really found those to be good lessons from peer to peer.

Of course, some students gave in and let a student that was a little short on tickets, perhaps to buy a 20-ticket bag of chips, have the tickets. Some students bought for others, only with a reminder, "You owe me." Real life lessons were being taught from the **"THE CLASS STORE."**

I really tried hard to make each day a great day for my students. We even had a CLASS PLEDGE that helped start each day of their class period. It was a way of helping students, "Clean the junk from the trunk" before class started. They had to say it EVERYDAY!! Eventually, we put the pledge to a "musical beat" and they wanted to "RAP" it daily. Kids, who are now adults, still come up to me and say, "I remember the CLASS PLEDGE."

THE CLASS PLEDGE

Today is a new day,

I am glad about this day,

What I did yesterday is gone,

Today, I can make a fresh start,

I expect good things to happen to me,

I believe it,

I conceive it,

I WILL achieve it,

I can do it,

I can do it,

I WILL do it!!

Written by Felecia George Prince, 2005

I didn't like boredom and I was going to find ways to make each day interesting and exciting. When the store was open, that day was far from being boring because shopping was going on in **"THE CLASS STORE" and that was FUN!!!**

There were always great stories and things to experience from the store. Some of the stories were funny, especially when a student bought a neat, little candle holder, but thought it was a cup. I saw her pouring a little soda in the glass and turning it up, so I politely said, "Sweetheart, that's a candleholder." She quickly put it away and wrapped it to take home.

Some of the stories were sad, especially when a student bought a one-of-a-kind item and it broke. I always felt so sorry for that student because the student was sad. Then, there were those memorable events where a student made some bad decisions and racked up on fines. This was the case with one of my students. Within the time period before the store opened, he had a total of about 200 to 300 fines. Unfortunately, this wasn't strange because I would have a few that "outperformed" others daily. Remember, I taught middle school.

One time, I had two students who were caught running in my classroom and broke my lamp. Since the lamp costed me $7, I charged them a 750-ticket fine. I had to add the 50 for running and playing. I didn't have any more broken lamps or anything else from them. One of them made some changes and earned enough bucks to shop in the next store. What a success story.

Every once in a while when a student received a LOT of fines, I heard the words, "Oh, you just want to say, FINE FINE FINE! You want to take all my tickets." I always quickly responded by saying as respectfully as I could, "I don't want to give you a fine. Actually, I didn't give it; you earned the fine. I don't want you to lose your tickets. I WANT you to shop."

One memorable event occurred with a student who made some really inappropriate choices. Within the time period before the store opened, the student had a total of 300 or more fines. Now, it was shopping day and the student wanted to make a purchase. The student asked for a second chance, but I made it plain and reminded the student that there were procedures prior to shopping and these procedures were well-explained and understood at the beginning. Those fines were the result of the choices made. Of course, the student wasn't happy. Actually, I felt sorry for the student, but I knew allowing the student to shop would not teach a good lesson. The student sat in agony watching others shop and buy things, such as candy, chips, games, key chains, and other gifts. The student went back and forth asking to please shop. My answer was still the same, in love, "Honey, I can't. You have to pay your bills. You made the choice to continue to accumulate fines even after reminders about talking, being disrespectful to peers, being off task, and using inappropriate language." After the student realized I wasn't giving in to the sad looks and begs, the student devised a plan.

"Ms. Prince, I really want these three things," said my little student as he held the key chain, key finder, and large box of chocolate candy in his hand. Let me PLEASE put them on layaway." Now, this wasn't a strange request for me because I had been asked before by others.

I listened, but I quickly responded to the student with words I am sure weren't welcoming to his ear, "I can't allow you to use layaway. Sweetheart, you owe a bill. The same bucks you are using for layaway, you need to use them to pay your bill. I can't allow you to use layaway or make partial payments when you owe a bill. Pay your bill in full first." In actuality, the student didn't even have enough bucks for layaway or to put the items on hold.

So, that day, the student went around asking for others to help out. The student even volunteered to work for some extra bucks, as many students have done.

The store did that. It brought out GREAT work ethics in many students. I didn't have to repeat and repeat the words, "Clean up." They didn't mind volunteering, especially during the store week.

"Ms. Prince, can I work for some bucks?" The student was able to come up with enough bucks to pay off the bill, leaving only enough for the 10% down on his layaway items, which costed 75 Princebucks. The layaway items were kept secured in a small drawer.

It took a few weeks for the student to earn tickets. By that time, the day came for the store to reopen. The student was ready to shop! Instead of all the items he had placed on layaway, he went with something different from the store. This actually turned out WONDERFUL for **more than one reason!**

One day, as it happened each year, little mice entered our school building from a nearby wooded area. Unfortunately, one entered the small drawer where the student's layaway was located and feasted on the student's candy. The items had to be discarded. The student never knew the layaway became lunch for a little animal. This was a wonderful story all the way around. The student was able to shop for a tasty treat. I didn't have to break the bad news about his layaway, and a little animal possibly received its last supper. Again, things turned out good for **more than one reason.**

COST OF FINES: Fines may have different costs. You can set your own prices. Below are some fines and prices I have used in the past. I didn't try to collect fines immediately, I just marked by the name or violation on my clipboard and kept it moving. Keeping good documentation really holds students accountable. If a student seemed NOT to remember she received a fine, I politely took out my clipboard and read, "On

August 1st during 3rd block, you said the "S" word.

The "S" word was "SHUT-UP." The "S" word was a curse word in my class. The kids quickly said, "Don't use the "S" word. Ms. Prince doesn't like that word. Saying the "S" word costed "25-tickets" each time it came from a student's mouth.

Now, I allowed students 3-5 seconds to say, "I am sorry." As one student said, "Ms. Prince, it's a habit. I can't help it. I am used to saying it." Well, I reminded her that she had to work at it, because she received a 25-ticket fine each time. She did learn quickly."

About three days before the store opened, fine bills or notices were issued. I always tried to place them in an envelope and pass them out to students who owed a fine. Sometimes, I just read from my clipboard. I worked to keep it professional. The envelope served two purposes, for students to receive their bill and place their tickets or bucks in, along with the bill receipt.

CIA

Document when students are issued a fine because they will act as if they just can't remember. Below are some examples of fines and prices:

Action	Tickets/bucks
Talking	3
Saying the "S" (Shut up) word without an immediate "I'm sorry"	25
Out of desk	3
Incomplete assignment	3
Off task	3

Action	Tickets/bucks
Horse playing	3
Inappropriate language	3
Obstruction or destruction of others property	10+

All fines had to be paid in FULL before the student could shop. **"We count tickets; not cash."** I had to remind them of this because they might ask to pay in cash.

Chapter 7

The store is open? When can I shop? It's shopping day?

Answer: "You can start shopping today if you have no fines. Once all your fines are paid, you can then shop."

Daily, I constantly reviewed and warned students about fines and acquiring tickets. "The store will open in about three weeks." **"THE CLASS STORE"** is coming. "Get ready, the store will be opening soon." I probably sounded like Paul Revere, saying "The British are coming." Overall, it was exciting for me! I loved to remind them because most of my students got excited also. This was a unique classroom experience. To answer the question of "When will the store be opened?" I also included it on their calendar agenda each week for reminders and wrote it on the board.

Setting Up the Store

Before the opening day, I displayed all items with sticky note prices. I used a basic set up for the small space within my classroom. I used crates and wooden stools as props to build upward. Vertical height moved the eyes up and down, signifying strength and power. I wanted the store's display to capture the attention of the students, and it did!

Students anticipated the arrival of the store as they approached because they saw signs posted saying, "THE STORE IS OPEN!" Sometimes, they saw me from afar waving a big sign that read "THE STORE IS OPEN!" Again, this generated excitement for the great activity they were about to partake in.

Another idea for involving student creativity is to have students design the store as an art project referred to as the "Store Design Contest." Then, the store setup can follow the winning sketch and that designer was charged with setting up the store. This is another method of encouraging students to buy in and take ownership of their class store.

CIA
Suggestions or ideas for store set-up:
- Student store design contest
- Store tag design
- Shopping bag design
- Student volunteer
- Parent volunteer

Encourage student participation by letting them create the store design. A "Store Design Contest" can be implemented. Then, the store setup can follow the winning sketch and that designer would be in charge of setting up the store.

Also, students can participate in other designs of the store, such as the store sign, tag designs, shopping bag designs, and even designing the "bucks." Encouraging student participation will motivate students to "buy-in" to the activities of **THE CLASS STORE."**

THE CLASS STORE

CIA
THE CLASS STORE suggested materials or supplies are as follows:
- bucks or tickets
- tables
- envelopes

- scissors
- printer
- shelves
- bill receipts
- store items
- class rosters
- black Sharpie
- sticky notes or price labels
- pen
- tape
- crates
- glue gun
- shredder or trash can
- cleaning supplies
- extra drawers
- zip lock bags

TIME TO SHOP

To keep things peaceful and systematic, I only allowed students to shop during their block in my class. There were four blocks and each block of students had their shopping time. The first day of shopping was for the students who had NO fines at all. It was like a "NO FINE PREFERRED SHOPPER'S DAY." This was an incentive for those who had clean slates, or NO FINES for the whole time. These students really enjoyed shopping first because they received FIRST CHOICE.

They knew the store had some "one-of-a-kind items." These were some of the students that I had in mind with **"THE CLASS STORE"** design. So, they were able to shop first.

Next, students who had fines paid their bills or brought envelopes to me after the NO FINE SHOPPERS. Usually, I set a quota of three items for each day, until the last day. Sometimes I was even able to have a discount or sale on the last day.

In order to be fair, I usually allowed the store to remain open for three days, then it closed until the next store opening. I wanted to give all students ample shopping time.

STUDENTS SHARING BUCKS

Because I treated this system like parents receiving a paycheck, I allowed students the autonomy to make their own decisions with their hard-earned bucks. My comments were, "Can your parents choose to give their paycheck to a neighbor?" The students replied, "Yes ma'am! It's their choice." So, I let them know sharing was their choice, but the consequence could mean less buying for them.

Also, this topic led to other discussions where the students realized some people only tried to use them for their bucks. Several of the students in response shared, "They still don't want to be your friend; they just want your bucks." Like it or not, **"THE CLASS STORE"** simulated "Real World" discussions and as their teacher, I tried to allow the students to work through these tough thoughts and just facilitate where needed.

If I received a buck from one student with another students' name, that student would have to personally write a note saying he or she gave the other student permission to use the buck. Professionalism was incorporated at all times! Students were driven to exemplify the respect and appreciation for the store as well as what **"THE CLASS STORE"** actually represented.

Chapter 8

The store is closed. When will it open again?

Answer: "Yes, the store is closed. Look at your calendar to find when it opens again."

Just as in life, everything comes to an end, whether good or bad. Even though the students knew the last shopping day ahead of time, that didn't stop them from asking the question. I was prepared to answer when asked, "Ms. Prince, the store has closed?" "We can't shop now?" "When will it open again?"

These were wonderful questions and a great time to discuss their experiences shopping at the store. The most profound question for me to ask was, "Did you enjoy shopping?"

As a middle school teacher, asking any question may result in a response you may not expect or want to hear. Overall, the conversation was positive. Some students shared concerns about the prices like, "I think the chips need to be about 10 tickets, not 20 or 30." "I couldn't shop because I lost all my tickets." "You need to buy more this or that." These statements from the kids led to strong, teachable moments. My response was, "Students, the prices will remain challenging because I allow you to earn lots of tickets or bucks throughout the weeks before the store opens." I continue with, "You must think of your bucks in terms of the economy; there are scarcities in life. You will probably not have all the bucks you would like. Let's face it, do your parents or even you, have all the money you want? Because of these reasons, it's so crucial to think about the decisions you make with the resources you do have. Actually, it's all about making great choices and managing your goods and services because you can't be sure that those goods will replenish." Again, these moments after the store closing were good times to teach those "life lessons." It was a wonderful time to listen and gather new ways to improve on the store's next opening. I would compare this time to when a server at a restaurant or phone service representative asks you to fill out a comment card about the service received. To me, this is one of the most important times of all, the grade after the test. The right questions could lead to improved ideas and experiences. Also, this encourages the students to collaborate and engage in the planning process of the store. For me as a teacher, it was rewarding to receive their feedback and input; but most importantly, it opened up a great opportunity for me to "LISTEN," which is another powerful tool to connect and build relationships with students or kids as a whole.

I believe the students learn and appreciate things more when they have opportunities to be involved in the learning process. "Student involvement" was often the case and highly encouraged in my class, especially through the sounds of MUSIC.

Social studies rocked in my classroom! As a social studies teacher and musician, there was always singing because we turned standards and lessons into musical lyrics! It was as simple as going to the keyboard in my classroom and turning on a beat. Below is a rap I created. It is called, **"THE CLASS STORE RAP."** Music can be motivating for many students. Also, teaching with music helps make learning fun and memorable.

I wrote this rap for this book. As the words explain, it was all about shopping at **"THE CLASS STORE."** It also reminds shoppers that they must earn their shopping privilege.

THE CLASS STORE RAP

BY

FELECIA GEORGE PRINCE

WRITTEN 6/12/2019

(Use a basic drumbeat created by the students. (Some love to beat on the desk anyway.))

I'M NOT GOING TO LOSE MY TICKETS,
I'M NOT GOING TO GIVE THEM AWAY,
'CAUSE I HAVE EARNED MY PLACE,
TO SHOP AT THE CLASS STORE.

I'M NOT GOING TO LOSE MY TICKETS,
I'M NOT GOING TO GIVE THEM AWAY,

'CAUSE I HAVE EARNED MY PLACE,
TO SHOP AT THE CLASS STORE.

I'M GOING SHOPPING TODAY,
I'M GOING SHOPPING TODAY,
I'M GOING SHOPPING TODAY,
IN THE CLASS STORE.

I'M GOING SHOPPING TODAY,
I'M GOING SHOPPING TODAY,
I'M GOING SHOPPING TODAY,
IN THE CLASS STORE.

YOU CAN EARN YOUR TICKETS,
YOU CAN EARN YOUR PLACE,
YOU CAN EARN YOUR TICKETS,
TO SHOP IN THE CLASS STORE.

YOU CAN EARN YOUR TICKETS,
YOU CAN EARN YOUR PLACE,
YOU CAN EARN YOUR TICKETS,
TO SHOP IN THE CLASS STORE.

I'M GOING SHOPPING TODAY,
I'M GOING SHOPPING TODAY,

I'M GOING SHOPPING TODAY,
IN THE CLASS STORE.

I'M GOING SHOPPING TODAY,
I'M GOING SHOPPING TODAY,
I'M GOING SHOPPING TODAY,
IN THE CLASS STORE.

YEAH!

SUMMARY

I hope you found this book to be motivating and useful. But more than anything, I hope you can see and feel the "LOVE." Love radiates from **"THE CLASS STORE."**

ABOUT THE AUTHOR

Felecia George Prince

Felecia George Prince is a native of Metter, Georgia. She was born in Savannah, GA, into a family of educators. Her mother, Ruthie George, is a retired teacher and her father, William E. George, Jr., is a retired principal. Felecia was educated in the Candler County School System. After finishing high school in 1982, she attended East Georgia College in Swainsboro,

Georgia, then West Georgia College (now West Georgia University) in Carrolton, GA. After a year, she transferred to Georgia Southern College (now Georgia Southern University) and pursued a Degree in Home Economics, Clothing and Textiles, Fashion and Designs. Shortly after graduation and spending three months in Atlanta, Felecia returned to Metter. She obtained a Middle Grades Certification and taught at Metter Middle School for five years under the leadership of her father. After those five years, she taught for three years on the campus of Georgia Southern University at Marvin Pittman Middle School. Then, she spent over 22 years teaching at William James Middle School before retiring on May 29, 2019. At William James, Felecia taught sixth and seventh grade social studies.

Felecia holds several memberships in various organizations, and she is a member of the Historic Mt. Pleasant Missionary Baptist Church in Claxton, GA, where she serves as Minister of Music. She also serves as youth musician and Sunday school teacher on first Sundays. She has been a musician for over 50 years.

In addition to holding a master's degree in education from Troy University, Felecia is presently completing a Doctorate Degree in Teacher Leadership at Walden University. Her research focuses on differentiated instruction.

Felecia is the mother of Jalen Prince, born on Christmas of 1996. Jalen was a 2015 Honors of Merit Graduate from Metter High School and is presently a Sport's Management Major at Georgia Southern University. Felecia is also "Auntie-Mom" of

Caleb Green, a 2016 Honors of Excellent Graduate from Metter High School and the Bill Gates Award Recipient for 2016. Presently, Caleb attends Claflin University in Orangeburg, South Carolina.

As a creative writer, Felecia loves to inspire and motivate. She is a monthly columnist for the *Metter Advertiser Newspaper*. Her column is entitled "THE ASSIGNMENT." She has a passion for education, and she loves teaching. Felecia frequently incorporates music in her lessons, which has become a powerful instructional strategy to help students learn. **She believes that effective teaching is all about having the fruit of the spirit and a gift from God.**

Felecia can be contacted via the following information, and she is available to conduct workshops:

feleciap@ymail.com
feleciaprince3@gmail.com
reachteachloves.com
Phone: 912-362-0804

634 NE Main St, #1263
Simpsonville, SC 29681
HadassahsCrown@gmail.com
864-708-1214
"Publishing Excellence With Integrity"

www.ingramcontent.com/pod-product-compliance
Lightning Source LLC
Chambersburg PA
CBHW052159110526
44591CB00012B/2007